FOCUS ON

LIGHT

BARBARA TAYLOR

SHOOTING STAR PRESS

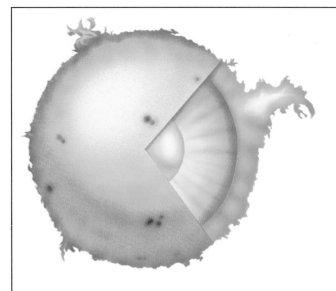

This edition produced in **1993** for
Shooting Star Press Inc
230 Fifth Avenue
New York, NY 10001

Design	David West Children's Book Design
Designer	Flick Killerby
Series Director	Bibby Whittaker
Editors	Suzanne Melia
	Elise Bradbury
Picture research	Emma Krikler
Illustrators	Simon Tegg
	Dave Burroughs
	Karen Johnson

Created and produced by
Aladdin Books Ltd
28 Percy Street
London W1P 9FF

*First published in the
United States in 1992 by*
Gloucester Press

ISBN 1-56924-033-7

Printed in Belgium

INTRODUCTION

Light illuminates our world. It brings us color and makes it possible for us to see. More importantly, without light from the sun, life on Earth would not be possible. People have found ways to make and control light, and it is used for many purposes other than to see by. In the recent past, scientists have developed ways of using light which improve our quality of life, for example, laser surgery and fiber optics. In the following pages, the properties of light are examined, bringing in related information from other subjects like arts, geography, history, math, and literature. This approach will help you to understand not only scientific principles, but introduce you to other ways of looking at light as well.

Geography

The symbol of the earth highlights panels which contain geographical information. These explain how lasers are used to collect information about the planet, and look at how different cultures use light.

Language and literature

Look for the sign of the open book to find information on how light and darkness are portrayed in literature, to learn legends and myths about the origins of light, and to discover the symbolic role of light in our language.

Science
The microscope symbol indicates a science project or experiment, such as how to split light into its spectrum, and how to prove that light travels in straight lines. It also shows where additional scientific or natural history information is given.

History
The sign of the scroll and hourglass shows where historical information is included. These sections explore how people have generated light through the ages and how they explained light before scientific theories.

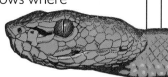

Math
Math projects and information are indicated by the symbol of a ruler and compass. These panels will increase knowledge about light and vision with hands-on activities, for example, measuring shadows to tell the time.

Art
The symbol showing art tools signals art activities, like creating shadow theater and experiments with mixing color. These aim to make learning science fun, and will cultivate creativity and imagination.

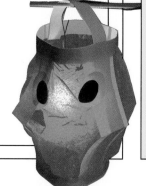

CONTENTS

LIGHT ALL AROUND

Nearly all the earth's light comes from our nearest star, the sun, which is a whirling cloud of very hot gases. These gases glow very brightly, emitting (giving out) light. All hot things give out light – even people, who emit invisible infrared light. Other natural sources of light on Earth come from lightning, fire, and the rest of the stars. Insects, such as fireflies, and some deep-sea fish, glow as a result of chemical reactions that release light. We can create artificial light by burning fuels in lamps, and by producing electricity for light bulbs.

Celebrations with light
Light has a special significance in cultures around the world, because it has long played an important role in human life. When people gather together to mark certain occasions, they might burn a bonfire or light candles.

Diwali
Diwali is the Hindu festival of light. It is celebrated at the end of the year as a victory of good over evil. Hindus light divas (lamps) for the occasion.

Independence Day
On July 4th in the United States, people celebrate their country's independence from British colonial rule by holding great firework displays.

Christmas
Millions of people around the world celebrate Christmas. Some decorate trees with strings of electric lights. Others light candles, and may set fire to a traditional Christmas pudding.

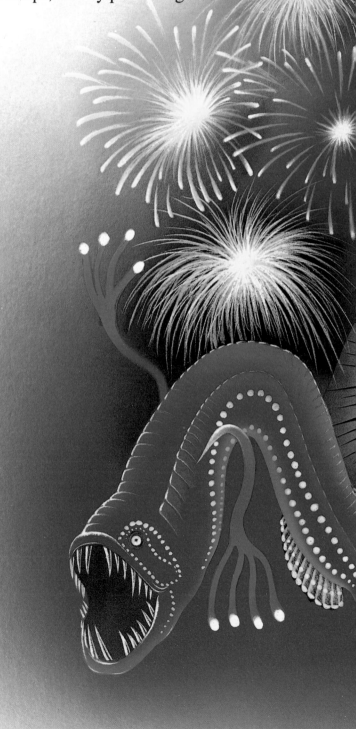

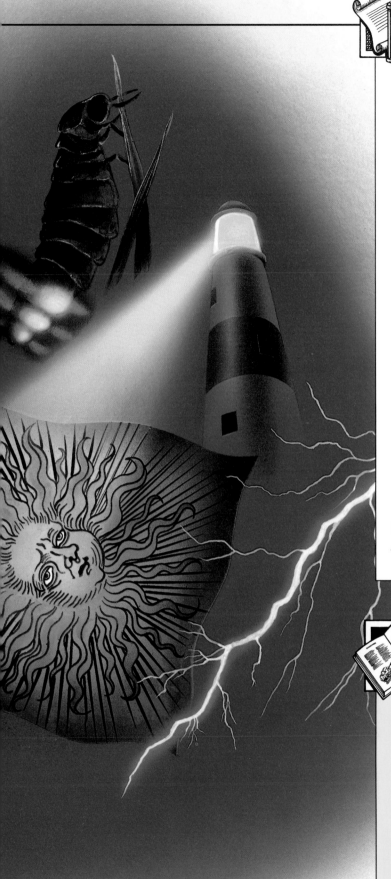

One of the most important things that sets human beings apart from other animals, is their ability to make and use tools. At the point when humans found they could make fire by rubbing sticks or flint stones together, they began to control their environment. There is evidence of humans using fire hundreds of thousands of years ago. Fire was used for cooking, for heat, for making tools, and was also used for illumination. Cave dwellers made lamps of burning animal fat in order to see inside dark caves. These lamps enabled them to paint pictures on the cave walls.

Shedding light on language
Words often carry meanings which are more than just their literal definition. "Light" has come to mean more than just visible brightness. Our language uses it to describe happiness; someone's "face lit up" and to symbolize truth; they "saw the light." Sunlight and daylight are often considered to be inspirational, hence the phrase "It dawned on me." "Dark," on the other hand, is often associated with the night, and all things bad and sinister. See if you can compose a story or poem using the symbolic meanings of light and dark.

WHAT IS LIGHT?

Light is a mixture of electrical and magnetic energy that travels faster than anything else in the universe. It takes less than one tenth of a second for light to travel from New York to London. Light is made up of tiny particles of energy called photons. The light moves along in very small waves that travel forward in straight lines, called rays. Light can travel through air and transparent substances, but can also travel through empty space. This is how sunlight reaches the earth. Light is similar to other forms of electromagnetic energy which have different wavelengths.

Radio waves
These have the longest wavelength. They are used for satellite communication and to carry TV and radio signals.

Visible light
Appears white or colorless, but is made up of colors, each with a different wavelength.

Radio	Micro	Infrared	Visible

Electromagnetic spectrum
This shows different kinds of electromagnetic energy arranged in order of their wavelengths. Wavelength is the distance between two consecutive waves.

Microwaves
Very short radio waves used in microwave ovens. They are also used in radar.

Infrared rays
Invisible rays, but we can feel the heat from them. They can be used to detect cancer and arthritis, or to take photographs in the dark.

Different ways of seeing
Most animals see visible light like we do. However, others have evolved sight which detects different wavelengths along the spectrum. Some insects see in ultraviolet light, which is invisible to most mammals and birds (except pigeons). Insect-pollinated flowers have lines which guide insects to their nectar. These lines only appear in ultraviolet light. The insects follow the guide lines to the nectar, scattering pollen on the way. This process helps the flowers to reproduce.

Bees cannot see the color red. They are strongly attracted by yellow and blue flowers which usually have strong ultraviolet markings. These markings attract bees to the flowers, and even pinpoint the location of the nectaries.

Ultraviolet rays

These cause us to tan and help the skin to produce vitamin D. Large amounts are dangerous and may cause skin cancer, although most ultraviolet light from the sun is absorbed by the ozone layer.

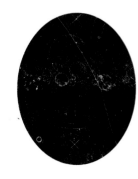

Gamma rays

These have the shortest wavelength. They are given off by naturally radioactive materials, such as uranium, and are part of the fallout after a nuclear explosion. They can travel through lead and cement, and damage living tissue.

UV	X rays	Gamma

X Rays

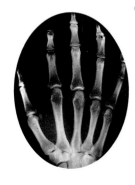

Called "X" by their discoverer because he was unsure of their nature. They pass through flesh, but are absorbed by bones and teeth, causing them to show up on x ray film. Small doses are safe, but large amounts are harmful to living tissue.

Taking the straight path

Try this experiment to prove that light travels in straight lines. Cut out two pieces of cardboard, about 8 in square. Make a hole in the center of each piece of scardboard, and stick a knitting needle through both holes, ensuring that they are aligned. Fix the cardboards onto a flat surface with modeling clay. Turn off the light and shine a flashlight through the holes. What happens? Try putting certain materials like cellophane, paper, or a book, between the two cards when the flashlight is on. Describe what happens to the ray of light.

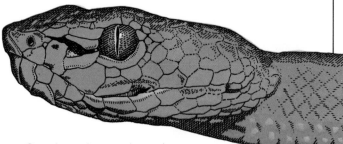

Certain snakes, such as pit vipers and pythons, detect prey by sensing the infrared light or "heat" they give out. They have special heat sensors which form an image from the infrared emissions. This helps them to hunt at night.

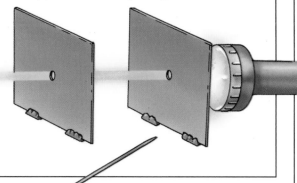

COLORS

Can you imagine a world without color? Some animals, such as horses and dogs, cannot see the colors we can. Their world is full of shades of black, white, and gray. We can see all the colors of visible light only when they have been separated out into their different wavelengths. Drops of water, raindrops, or specially shaped pieces of transparent material called prisms, can do this. As light passes through these things, each color is bent by a slightly different amount, emerging at the other side as a band of rainbow colors. This is called a spectrum. The colors always appear in the same order.

Primary colors

Most colors of light can be made by mixing together the three main colors. These are red, blue, and green. You can see these colors if you take a close look at the tiny dots of light on a television screen. These are called the primary colors of light, and are different from the primary colors of paint, which are magenta, yellow, and blue.

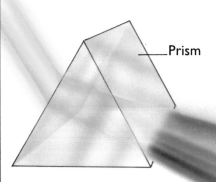

Prism

Violet light is bent the most.

Colors of the spectrum

"White light" can be separated into the colors of the spectrum. Make your own spectrum by putting a glass of water on a piece of white paper. Place this near a window in the morning or evening. Make a half inch slit in a piece of cardboard and tape it to the glass. The spectrum will appear on the paper.

Sun-light

Experimenting with paint

When colored paints are mixed together, they form a dark, black shade. This is because paint contains pigments which reflect certain colors when light shines on it. Try painting a picture using small dots of red, yellow, and blue. This technique is called pointillism. Look at the picture from a distance. Do the dots merge to form new colors?

Use a fine paint brush to create the dots. Crayons and felt tip pens are just as good.

Red sock in blue light

Red sock

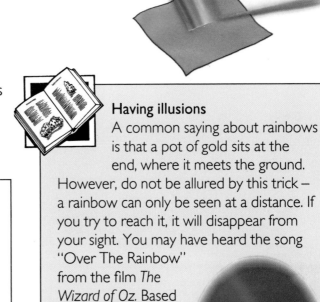

Reflecting color

The color you see when you look at an object is the color it reflects, or bounces back into your eyes. A red object reflects red light, and absorbs the other colors. An object looks white if it reflects all the different wavelengths of visible light. A black object absorbs all the colors, and reflects hardly any light.

Lost to history

Sir Isaac Newton (1642-1727) was an English mathematician and physicist, best known for his laws of motion and gravity. However, he also studied light, and was the first to prove light is made up of different colors. Ironically, a lit candle on Newton's desk burned 20 years' worth of his research papers on light and optics.

Having illusions

A common saying about rainbows is that a pot of gold sits at the end, where it meets the ground. However, do not be allured by this trick – a rainbow can only be seen at a distance. If you try to reach it, it will disappear from your sight. You may have heard the song "Over The Rainbow" from the film *The Wizard of Oz*. Based on L. Frank Baum's book *The Wonderful Wizard of Oz*, the story follows Dorothy's adventures in a fantasy land beyond the rainbow.

THE SUN AND STARS

For many millions of years, the sun has been giving out visible light and all the other forms of electromagnetic energy. The Sun is 93 million miles from the earth, but its electromagnetic energy travels so fast, it reaches us in only eight minutes. It moves at an amazing 985 million feet per second! Other stars are so far from the earth that their light takes millions of years to reach us. The planets and their moons do not produce light of their own like the stars. They appear to shine only when sunlight bounces off them.

How the sun makes light

The sun is incredibly hot, which makes the atoms in its gases move about a lot, crashing into each other. When hydrogen gas (A) bumps into more hydrogen gas (B), another gas called helium (C) is produced. This process is called nuclear fusion, and it releases huge amounts of electromagnetic energy (D), including light.

Core

Sunspots

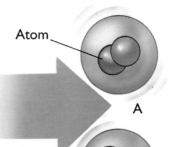

Atom

A

B

Atom

Food chains

Plants are the only living things that can make their own food. So animals have to eat plants – or other animals that have already eaten plants. A simple series of feeding links, such as grass-rabbit-fox, is called a food chain. The sun's energy is passed on at each link in the chain. Food chains join, forming a food web which can easily be upset if one link changes.

Carbon dioxide absorbed

Oxygen released

Water

Plant power

All life on Earth exists because plants are able to use the sun's energy to make their own food. This process is called photosynthesis, which means "making things with light." It takes place mainly in a plant's leaves. The sun's energy is trapped by a green pigment called chlorophyll, and used to join carbon dioxide and water to make sugars. Oxygen is released into the air as a waste product.

C

D

Solar power

Modern society relies on energy to function. It powers our cars, runs our factories, heats our homes, and cooks our food. At the moment we burn oil and gas to get much of our energy. However, the sun's rays carry enough energy to our planet to supply more than our present needs. Solar power can be used to heat water in our homes, or large solar power plants can be set up to provide electricity for towns and cities.

Reaching for the light

The sun's light is essential for plants to grow. When seeds germinate under the ground, they look for the light in a process known as geotropism. Plant a sprouting potato in a pot of moist soil, and put it at one end of a box. Place partitions along the box, as shown, and then make a hole at the opposite end from the plant. Put a lid on the box and place it somewhere sunny. After several days, the sprout will emerge from the hole. What conclusions can you draw from this?

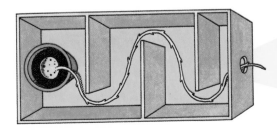

Sun worshippers

Most ancient cultures had a way of explaining phenomena that we now understand in scientific terms. These explanations are known as myths. Many ancient peoples worshipped the sun as a god. Some thought that an eclipse of the sun was the sun god's way of expressing anger.

Re

The ancient Egyptians worshipped the sun god Re, who carried the sun across the sky in a barge.

In ancient Greek mythology the sun was driven from east to west in a flaming chariot, guided by the sun god Helios. Can you think of any other myths about the sun?

Helios

OTHER SOURCES OF LIGHT

Apart from nuclear fusion, there are several other ways of making light. In light bulbs, electricity is passed through a thin coil of metal, which gets so hot it glows with a bright light. Sodium lights (yellow streetlamps) or the neon lights used in advertising, give out light when electricity is passed through a gas. Some plants and animals, such as fungi and fireflies, use chemical reactions to glow with light. This is called cold light, as it is emitted without high temperatures. Some rocks also glow with a cold light.

Life before the light bulb
Before the inventor Thomas Edison developed the light bulb in 1879, people had to find other ways to light up their homes and workplaces. During the Middle Ages in Europe (1200-1500), most people had to manage with natural light. A fire for cooking would produce some light, but not enough to work by. By the 1800s, candlelight was far more widespread. People also made use of oil lamps. In European cities, like London, gas street-lights were used, which had to be lit and extinguished each evening. By the 1880s, electric light was in general use by the majority of the public.

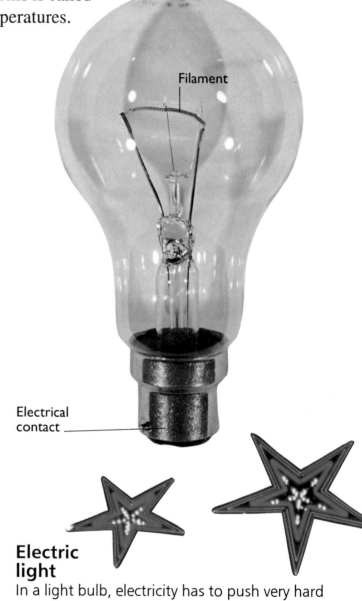

Filament

Electrical contact

Electric light

In a light bulb, electricity has to push very hard to move through an extremely long, thin wire. This pushing makes the wire so hot, it gives out light. Fluorescent lights are filled with mercury gas, which gives out invisible ultraviolet rays when electricity flows through it. These ultraviolet rays strike a coating of chemicals, called phosphors, on the inside of the tube, which then give out visible light. This is called fluorescence.

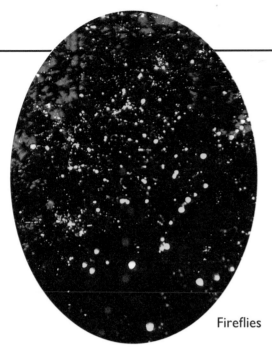
Fireflies

Chemical lights

Fireflies and glowworms flash their lights at
night, like a sort of Morse code, to find a mate
of the right species. Some deep-sea fish glow,
or carry groups of light-producing bacteria.
These help the fish to find food, to defend
themselves, or to attract mates.

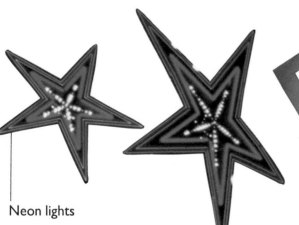
Neon lights

Glowworm lantern

Glowworms are
larvalike female
beetles. The male
adults of the species are called
fireflies. Both can glow or give
out flashing light. You can
make your own glowworm
lantern using colored tissue
paper, cardboard, and glue.

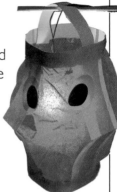

Wires

Fold a large piece of cardboard in
half lengthwise, and cut out some
wide slits at regular intervals. Now roll
one edge around to meet the
other and glue in
place. Line the
lantern with tissue,
and use a strip of
Bulb card for a
handle.

Make the
worm glow by
using a battery, a
small bulb, and two
pieces of long plastic
covered wire. Dangle
the bulb inside the
lantern from one end
of a stick.

Northern lights

Far from the equator, near the north
and south poles, curtains of colored
lights appear in the sky at certain times
of the year. These are caused by collisions
between particles that are sent out from huge
flares on the sun's surface. The lights, called
aurora borealis, are best seen from the northern
parts of Canada, Scotland, or Scandinavia. Similar
lights in the southern hemisphere are called
aurora australis.

LIGHT, DARK, & SHADOWS

The amount of sunlight reaching a place on Earth depends partly on the position of the earth in space, and its relation to the sun and the moon. It also depends on the curved surface of the earth and the way the whole planet tilts to one side. When the moon, sun and the earth are all in a straight line, the moon prevents some sunlight from reaching the earth. The shadow the moon causes makes some places on Earth dark during the day. This is called a solar eclipse. An eclipse of the moon occurs when the earth keeps sunlight from reaching the moon.

Sun

Earth

Shadow

The earth spins around (rotates) once every 24 hours. At night, your part of the earth is turned away from the sun, and is in shadow. The seasons happen because the earth is tilted at an angle. As it moves around the sun once a year, some places receive more light and heat.

Shadows form when objects block out light. Light cannot bend around the object because it travels in straight lines. The size of a shadow depends on the distance between the light and the object and the surface it falls on.

Measuring time from shadows

To make your own sundial you will need a piece of thin cardboard, a protractor, a compass, and a piece of thick cardboard. Cut out a triangle, as shown, from the thin cardboard. Make one angle a right angle (90°). Fold along the dotted line. With your compass, draw a semicircle on the thick cardboard. Fix the folded edge of the triangle to the cardboard, as shown, and place the sundial outside so the triangle points north-south. Every hour mark the position of the shadow on the base. Every day the shadow will travel the same distance, so you should be able to tell the time.

Mark each hour

8 in

90°   8 in

Opaque materials, like paper, act as a barrier to light, and will not let light pass through. Shadows form behind them.

Transparent materials, like glass, let light pass through. We can see through these materials, and they do not cast shadows.

Translucent materials, like tissue, let some light through. We cannot see clearly through these materials, and objects look blurred – they form faint shadows.

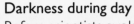

Darkness during day

Before scientists explained solar eclipses, some people thought they indicated the end of the world. Over 4,000 years ago, ancient Chinese myths held that an eclipse was a dragon trying to eat the sun. Their solution was to make as much noise as possible to scare the monster away, and the whole population would scream, bang gongs, and make a general uproar. However, they knew that eclipses followed certain patterns and were able to predict when they would occur.

Translucent

Opaque

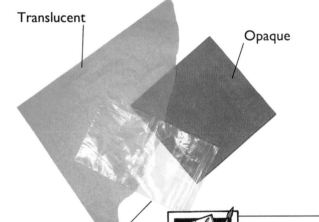

Transparent

Shadow theater

Shadow theater began in the Far East, in India and China. It is one of the oldest forms of theater in the world. All you need to put on your own shadow show is a light source directed at a flat, white surface. Using a white wall or a sheet of white paper as a backdrop, place a flashlight on a chair or table. For the characters of your show, use your hands to make different shapes, or cut out shapes and attach them to sticks. Use black paper or colored cellophane for a variety of results. For the best effect, make the room dark before you begin your theater.

Paper rods

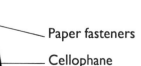

Paper fasteners

Cellophane

Black cardboard outline

REFLECTION

When light hits a surface, it bounces off again – rather like a ball bouncing off a wall. This is called reflection. Reflected light makes things sparkle and shine. Mirrors produce the best reflections, because they are smooth and flat, and reflect most of the light that strikes them. The image in a mirror is different from real life, because it is inverted (or reversed). You don't see yourself in a mirror as other people see you. Curved (or convex) mirrors can change the size of images, and concave mirrors (which curve inward) can turn images upside down.

Brilliant reflection
Birds' feathers vary from the dull-colored tones of a sparrow, to the bright plumage of a parrot. Blacks, grays, and browns result from pigments (colorings) in the feather itself. Yellow, orange, and red plumage, however, come from pigments obtained in the bird's diet. A flamingo is only pink because of the red brineshrimp it feeds on. Green, blue, and violet colored feathers are produced as light reflects off the structure of the feather. A peacock's iridescent plumage is created by light reflecting off microscopic fringes, called barbules, on each feather.

Peacock's
feather

Make a kaleidoscope
Kaleidoscopes form beautiful colored patterns which are always changing.
To make one, tape together three small mirrors of the same size (A). Make sure they are facing each other. Stand the mirrors upright on a piece of cardboard, and draw around the end with a pencil. Cut out this shape and tape it onto the mirrors. Now poke a hole through the cardboard (B). Tape a piece of tracing paper over the other end (C), and drop some colored beads or bits of paper through the hole. Look through the hole and point the other end toward the light. Move the kaleidoscope, and you will see a different pattern.

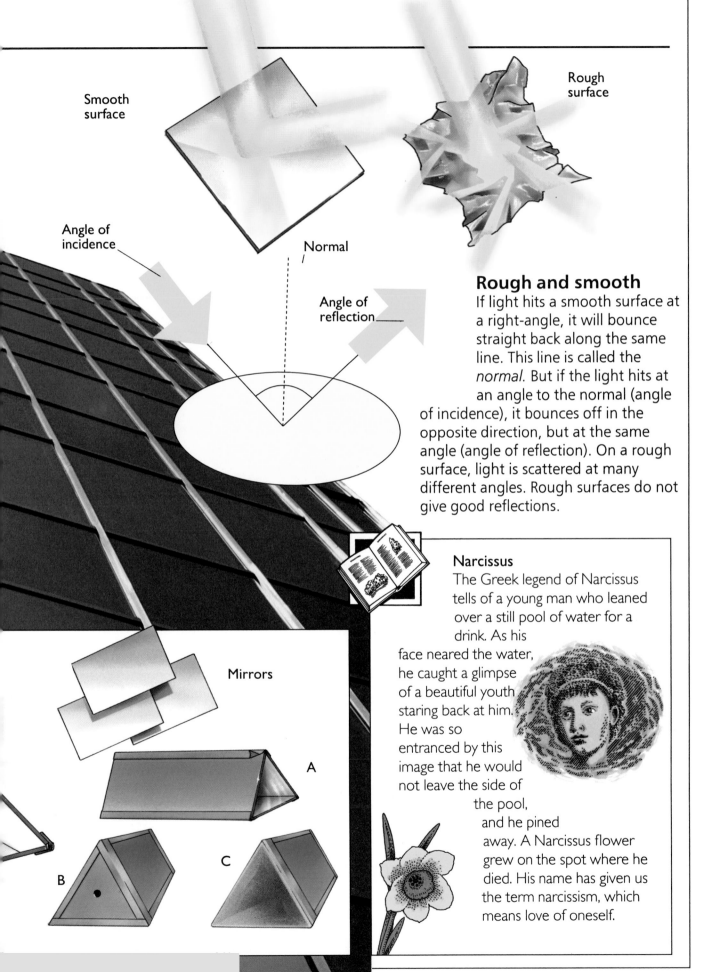

Smooth surface

Rough surface

Angle of incidence

Normal

Angle of reflection

Rough and smooth
If light hits a smooth surface at a right-angle, it will bounce straight back along the same line. This line is called the *normal*. But if the light hits at an angle to the normal (angle of incidence), it bounces off in the opposite direction, but at the same angle (angle of reflection). On a rough surface, light is scattered at many different angles. Rough surfaces do not give good reflections.

Mirrors

A

B

C

Narcissus
The Greek legend of Narcissus tells of a young man who leaned over a still pool of water for a drink. As his face neared the water, he caught a glimpse of a beautiful youth staring back at him. He was so entranced by this image that he would not leave the side of the pool, and he pined away. A Narcissus flower grew on the spot where he died. His name has given us the term narcissism, which means love of oneself.

REFRACTION

Light travels fastest through space, and moves more slowly through air. Water then slows light down further, by about 25 percent, and glass slows it down even more, by about 35 percent. When light passes from air to water or from air to glass, it slows down, causing it to change direction. This "bending" effect is called refraction. Swimming pools look shallower than they really are, because of the way the light from the bottom of the pool is refracted as it moves from the water into the air. Lenses refract light, and can make objects appear larger or smaller than they really are.

Convex lenses

Lenses are pieces of transparent material with a curved surface. Convex lenses curve outward on both sides. They bend the light rays inward, where they meet at the focus of the lens. They magnify (enlarge) things, and are used in spectacles to correct farsightedness.

Bending light

Cut two narrow slits, 1 in apart, at one end of a cardboard shoe box. Put a sheet of white paper in the bottom of the box, placing a jar of water on top. Now line up the jar with the slits. Turn off the light in the room, and shine a flashlight through the slits. Can you see the light bending through the water and meeting on the other side?

The power of light

Sunlight is extremely powerful. If concentrated onto one spot, it can cause fires. For centuries it has been known that light bending through a magnifying glass can set fire to wood. In the ruins of a city in ancient Mesopotamia (now Iraq), burning glasses have been found, dating back to the 7th century B.C. And in 1774, the scientist Lavoisier, used this knowledge to build "the great burning lens" with which he roasted a mixture of metal and charcoal. However, it's not just magnifying glasses that can concentrate light. Pieces of ordinary glass are also able to do this. If you go for a walk in a forest or wood, you may see signs that warn against the hazards of fire. Glass bottles are dangerous things to leave behind if you have a picnic. On a hot day, sunbeams through glass bottles may cause a fire to start.

The rays that produce mirages are real, and can be photographed.

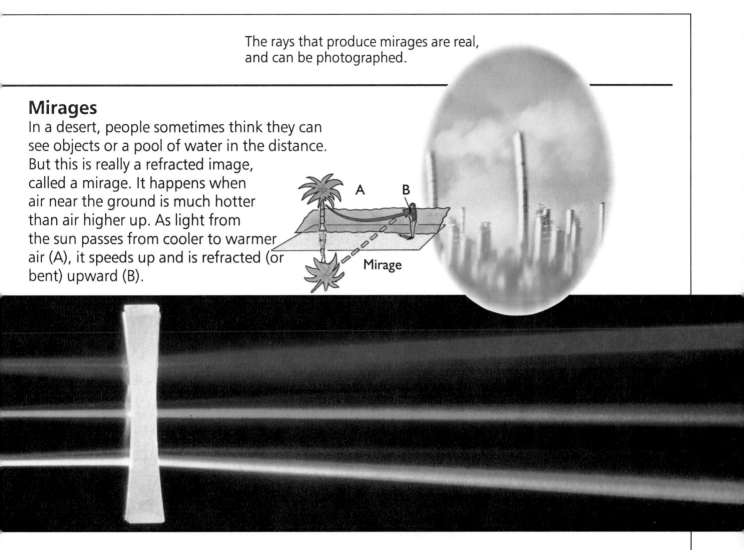

Mirages

In a desert, people sometimes think they can see objects or a pool of water in the distance. But this is really a refracted image, called a mirage. It happens when air near the ground is much hotter than air higher up. As light from the sun passes from cooler to warmer air (A), it speeds up and is refracted (or bent) upward (B).

Mirage

Concave lenses

Concave lenses curve inward on both sides. They make light rays bend outward or spread out. Concave lenses make things look smaller, and are used in the eyeglasses of nearsighted people, to correct their sight.

Lavoisier's burning glass was 52 ins in diameter. It comprised two sheets of glass, with the lens-shaped space between them filled with wine vinegar. Lavoisier is regarded as the founder of modern chemistry, and in 1772 he began a series of experiments that demonstrated the nature of combustion (burning).

Seeing things

At the north and south poles, the arctic cold creates mirages. A warmer layer of air (A) over a cold one, bends light rays (B) so that images appear where there is nothing. From a distance, ships can appear to be floating yards above the ocean's surface (C). At the end of the winter, after the long absence of the sun, a reflection of the sun can appear in a mirage days before it actually rises.

USING LENSES

Lenses are used to bend light in many instruments, from magnifying glasses and microscopes, to telescopes and binoculars. They also help us to see things that are too small or too far away for us to see with our eyes alone. Instruments that help us to see are called *optical*, from the Greek word for eye. The lenses in eyeglasses help people to see clearly when their eyes are not working properly. The lens in a camera brings the rays of light to a focus on the film, so a clear image is recorded. And the lenses in microscopes, telescopes, and binoculars make things look much larger than they really are.

The camera

A camera is a lightproof box with a hole at the front, called the aperture. A circular shutter usually stops light from getting inside. But when a photograph is being taken, the shutter opens for a split second to let light reach the film at the back. The film is coated with chemicals that are sensitive to light. The lens focuses the light to form an upside down image on the film. The amount of light hitting the film can be controlled by changing the aperture size or the shutter speed.

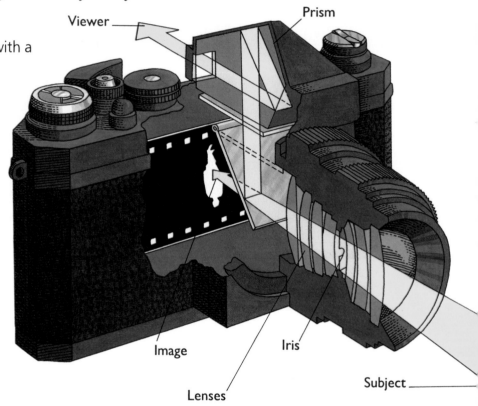

Viewer — Prism — Image — Iris — Subject — Lenses

Correcting vision

Sight is one of our most valuable senses. In the past, if you had less than perfect vision you would probably have had to be cared for by others. You could not hunt or keep an eye out for danger with blurry vision. As science progressed, people began to develop ways of correcting such problems as near- or farsightedness. Marco Polo, an Italian explorer, reported seeing people wearing glasses in China, in about 1275. The earliest known picture of eyeglasses was painted in Italy in 1352. Demand for reading glasses increased after printed books started to become available in the late 1400s. Since then, eyeglasses have become commonplace in modern society, with contact lenses becoming widely available in the 1960s.

Contact lens

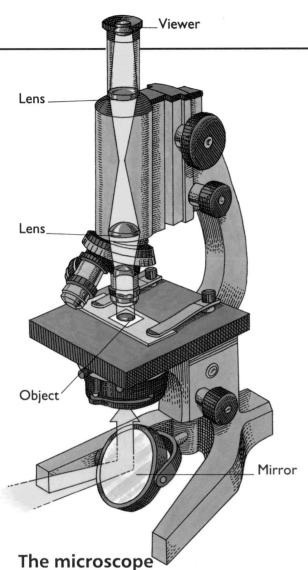

Viewer

Lens

Lens

Object

Mirror

The microscope
A light microscope is used to make very small things, such as minerals in rocks, or cells from living things, look hundreds of times bigger than they really are. This allows us to find out more about them. The objects are viewed from a very close distance. A mirror reflects light through the object, and convex lenses in the eyepiece and the body of the microscope magnify the image.

Do-it-yourself microscope
Microscope translates from Greek as "little watcher." You can make a basic microscope quite easily. You will need to place a thin glass upside down on a table, with a small mirror fixed at an angle inside it. Then take a thin strip of foil that has been folded several times, and punch a small hole in its center. Bend the edges of the foil so that it will fit over the base of the glass – use tape to stick it firmly. Insert a drop of water into the hole, and place a small insect on the base of the glass beneath it. The water will magnify this object up to 50 times its life size.

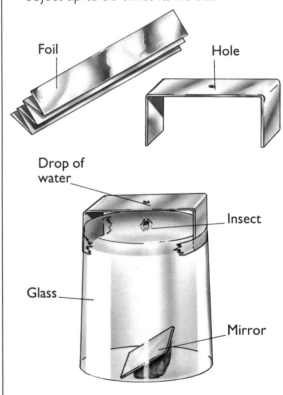

Foil

Hole

Drop of water

Insect

Glass

Mirror

Mirror, mirror on the wall...
Mirrors and lenses appear in literature in a variety of ways. The English writer, Lewis Carroll (1832-98), sends his heroine, Alice, to a fantastical location on the other side of her mirror in *Through the Looking-Glass.* Sherlock Holmes carries a magnifying glass at all times. Can you think of other examples of stories featuring mirrors or lenses?

EYES AND SEEING

Animals can see things when light is reflected into their eyes. Without light, it's impossible to see. The sense of sight is very important to animals, helping them to move about, find food and mates, and detect danger. Some animals, such as worms, can only see patches of light and dark. Others, such as humans and birds, have very good eyesight. The eye can see objects as far away as a star, and as tiny as a grain of sand. We can judge how far away things are from us and we can see in color. About four-fifths of the information our brain receives about our surroundings comes through our eyes.

Estimating distance with one eye

Test whether you need both eyes to judge distance properly with the following experiment. Close one eye, and estimate how far away from you an object is. Write down your guess. Now try again with both eyes open. Write this guess down as well. Then measure the distance accurately to see which guess was closer to the truth. If you try this experiment several times with a variety of objects, does your brain begin to make allowances for the loss of sight in one eye?

In nearsighted people, the light rays cross over in front of the retina.

In farsighted people, the light rays cross over behind the retina.

Iris expands and contracts to change the size of the pupil and control the amount of light entering the eye.

Conjuctiva

Vitreous humor

Pupil

The human eye

The eye is shaped like a ball with a lens inside, about the size of a pea. Light enters the eye through a hole called the pupil. The pupil is situated in the colored part of the eye, called the iris. Behind the iris is the soft, rubbery lens which focuses the light onto a layer, called the retina, at the back of the eye. The image on the retina is upside down, because the lens bends the light rays toward each other where they eventually cross over. This crossover point must fall exactly on the retina if we are to see a clear image. The retina contains light-sensitive chemicals which transform light into electrical messages. These messages are sent to the brain along the optic nerve, where they are turned the right-side up and "decoded."

Aqueous humor

Lens

Cornea

Muscles around the lens pull it into different shapes.

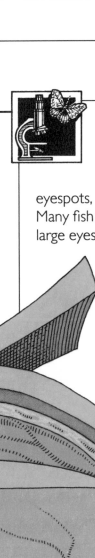

Other eyes

Not all animals have eyes which work like ours. Some invertebrates (animals without a backbone) have eyespots, which are small areas sensitive to light. Many fish and animals that hunt at night have large eyes and pupils. The tuatara of New Zealand, the oldest reptile in the world, has a third eye underneath a flap of skin on its forehead.

A chameleon's eyes stand out from its head and can move completely independently of each other. Spiders have 6-8 eyes to give them all around vision.

Insects and crustaceans have compound eyes which receive images in fragments, like a mosaic. These eyes are made up of many tiny lenses that see one bit of the total scene. All the bits combine to form an image.

Vertebrates can operate in a range of light intensities by adjusting the amount of light admitted through a pupil. A gecko's pupil can close to leave just a few pinholelike openings.

Blind spot, where there is no room for light-sensitive cells.

Image

Rods

Cones

Optic nerve

Retina

The cells in the retina are called rods and cones, because of their shape.
Rods work well in dim light and pick up shades of gray. There are about 125 million rods in each eye.
Cones work well in bright light and pick up colors. There are about 7 million cones in each eye.

Chloroid

Muscle

Up to the eyeballs

We use many expressions which contain references to the eyes. To "keep your eyes peeled" is to keep a lookout. If two people "see eye to eye" then they agree with each other. If a person "turns a blind eye," it means they are ignoring something. "In the mind's eye" refers to the imagination. Can you think of some other expressions, stories, or songs which use the eyes to convey meaning? Perhaps you could invent some new ones?

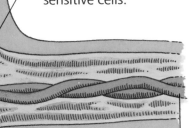

TRICK OF THE LIGHT

The human brain tries to make sense of the information detected by our eyes. To do this, it compares the information with its memory banks of previous experiences, using clues such as colors, shadows, shapes, and perspective. But the brain can be tricked by "puzzle pictures." These may have two or more possible meanings. The brain cannot decide which to choose, and we "see" first one interpretation and then another. The brain cannot make sense of these artificial pictures.

Movies
Moving pictures are a series of still pictures that we see one after the other. Movies have 24 pictures a second. They merge together to create an illusion of movement.

The first "movies"
The first moving picture is credited to Edweard Muybridge in 1877. He set up 12 cameras along intervals of a racetrack. As the racehorse passed by, it triggered the cameras, setting off each one in turn. The Victorians invented a device, called a praxinoscope, to show these sequences of photographs. It was basically a cylinder of photographs which was spun quickly. By looking through a slit, the spectator could see the pictures "move."

Viewing slits

Cut out a disk of cardboard about 8 in across. Draw your pictures around the edge, and cut out the viewing slits as shown. Push a nail through the center of the disk and into a cork. Put a bead either side of the disk to make it run smoothly. Now hold the disk up to a mirror with a good light behind you. Twirl the disk by gently striking the edge, and look through the slits. Watch the moving pictures in the mirror.

Muybridge's strip

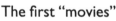

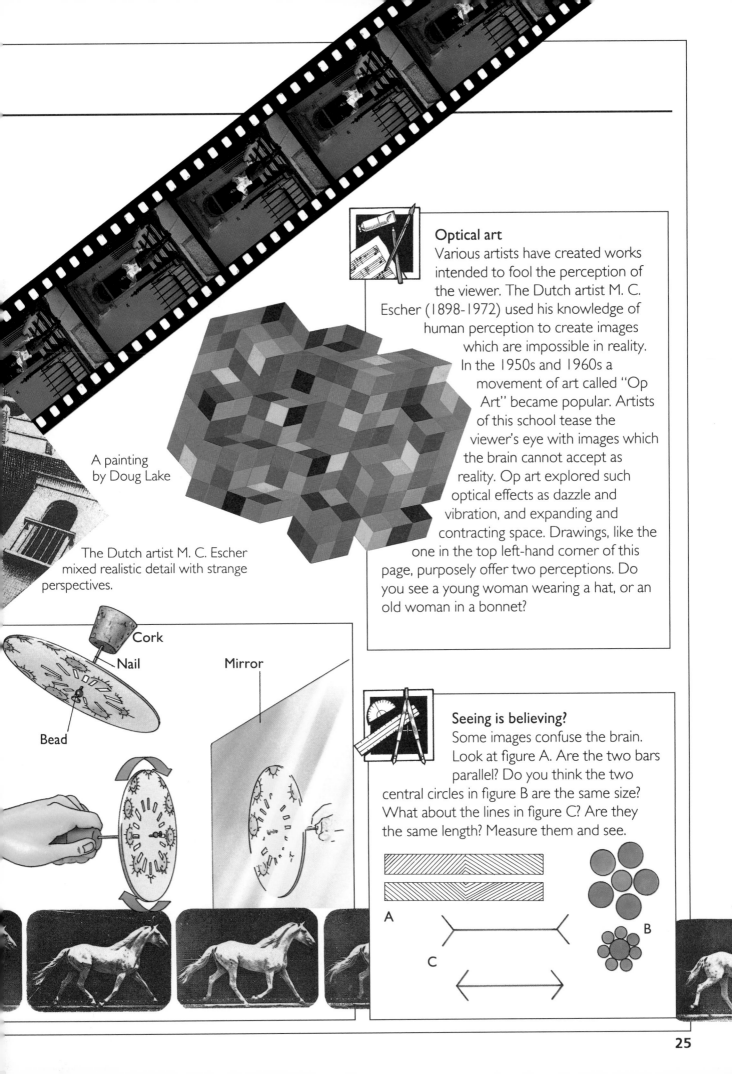

Optical art
Various artists have created works intended to fool the perception of the viewer. The Dutch artist M. C. Escher (1898-1972) used his knowledge of human perception to create images which are impossible in reality. In the 1950s and 1960s a movement of art called "Op Art" became popular. Artists of this school tease the viewer's eye with images which the brain cannot accept as reality. Op art explored such optical effects as dazzle and vibration, and expanding and contracting space. Drawings, like the one in the top left-hand corner of this page, purposely offer two perceptions. Do you see a young woman wearing a hat, or an old woman in a bonnet?

A painting by Doug Lake

The Dutch artist M. C. Escher mixed realistic detail with strange perspectives.

Cork

Nail

Mirror

Bead

Seeing is believing?
Some images confuse the brain. Look at figure A. Are the two bars parallel? Do you think the two central circles in figure B are the same size? What about the lines in figure C? Are they the same length? Measure them and see.

A

B

C

LASERS

A laser is a machine which turns an ordinary beam of light into a straight, narrow beam of very bright light. Laser light does not spread out like ordinary light, so it is concentrated and very powerful. It can cut through steel and human tissue, and can be used to measure distances accurately, make holograms and compact discs, or guide missiles. Lasers may produce visible light of one color only, or invisible infrared rays. All the waves are in step, and reinforce each other, which is why they are so powerful, and can travel long distances without fading.

Inside a laser is a tube filled with a gas, a solid, or a liquid, called the active medium. Usually, this is a man-made crystal, like ruby. Energy, such as light or an electric current, is passed through the active medium, making it give off light. Some of this bounces back and forth between two mirrors, making the active medium give off even more light. This is called lasing.

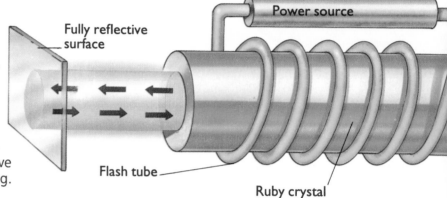

Power source

Fully reflective surface

Flash tube

Ruby crystal

Investigating the earth

Lasers have been very useful in increasing knowledge about our planet. The distance from the moon to the earth was measured by bouncing a laser beam off a reflector on the moon. Lasers, reflected off satellites orbiting the earth, can also detect tiny land movements on our planet. Scientists can use this data to measure the movements of continents or to detect earthquakes and volcanic eruptions.

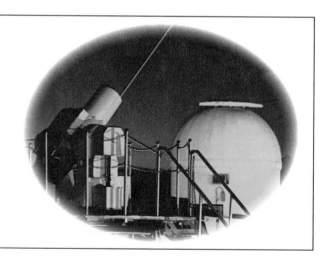

Futuristic weapons

Although laser weapons are relatively new on the scene in real life, imaginative science fiction writers and filmmakers have incorporated lasers into their works for a long time. Laser weapons appear in the James Bond movie, *Goldfinger* (1964) which was based on a book by Ian Fleming (1908-1964). Lasers also feature in the movie *Star Wars* (1977), where they are fired from guns and used as swords.

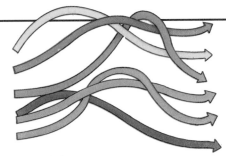

Ordinary light waves

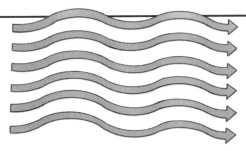

Laser light waves

Partially reflective surface

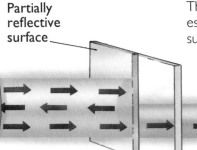

The beam of concentrated light then escapes through the partially mirrored surface, emerging as a laser beam.

Laser beam

Holograms

A laser beam can be used to record a ghostlike three dimensional image called a hologram. The laser beam (1) is split into two parts. One part is aimed at the object (2), and the reflected light, called the object beam, illuminates the film (3). The reference beam (4), is aimed directly at the film, forming a complex pattern. In figure B a beam of light identical to the reference beam (1) is directed at the developed film. A viewer (2) sees the image (3) in three dimensions.

History of the laser
The first laser was developed in 1960 by a scientist called T.H. Maiman.

1961 First commercially-built laser sold.
1961 First laser holograms developed.
1963 Lasers first used in surgery.
1966 Optical fibers using lasers developed.
1976 Lasers used to measure Earth's movements.
1982 Compact discs launched.
1988 First transatlantic optical fiber sends telephone messages.
1991 Laser-guided missiles used by U.S.A. in the Gulf War.
1992 Research into laser fusion continues.

Hologram

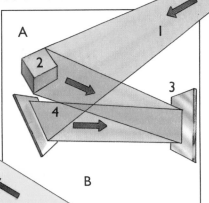

A = Recorded image

B = Viewing image

LIGHT LINKS

Flashes of light can be used to send messages in the form of a code. Light can be sent along hair-thin fibers of very pure glass, to carry messages such as telephone calls, computer data, or television broadcasts. These are called optical fibers, and they are so small and thin that they fit easily inside delicate instruments, called endoscopes. Doctors use endoscopes to see inside the human body. One thin fiber can also carry thousands of telephone conversations at the same time. At the other end of the fiber, the flashes of light are turned into electrical signals, which can be turned back into sound again.

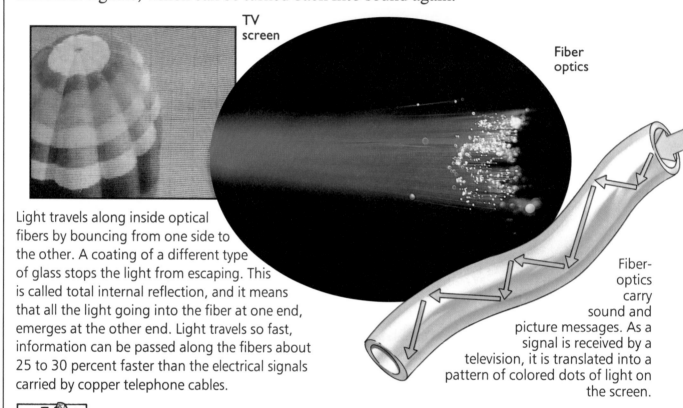

TV screen

Fiber optics

Light travels along inside optical fibers by bouncing from one side to the other. A coating of a different type of glass stops the light from escaping. This is called total internal reflection, and it means that all the light going into the fiber at one end, emerges at the other end. Light travels so fast, information can be passed along the fibers about 25 to 30 percent faster than the electrical signals carried by copper telephone cables.

Fiber-optics carry sound and picture messages. As a signal is received by a television, it is translated into a pattern of colored dots of light on the screen.

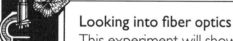

Looking into fiber optics
This experiment will show how light is reflected through the thin glass rods used in optical fibers. Find a large plastic bottle and make a hole in one side of it. Holding the bottle over a sink, fill it with water and quickly put on the top. Turn off the light in the room and ask someone to shine a flashlight on it, as shown. Put your finger in the stream of water pouring from the hole. What do you see on the end of your finger? The diagram above helps to explain how light is carried by the stream of water and by optical fibers. Light can travel around twists and curves by this method.

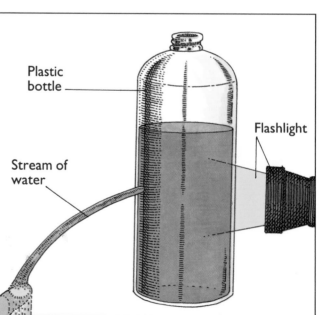

Plastic bottle

Flashlight

Stream of water

Communicating with light

Light is an effective form of communication over long distances. Lighthouses have warned sailors of dangers for thousands of years. The ancient Greeks were among the first people to use light to guide ships. The Pharos of Alexandria was the tallest lighthouse ever constructed, and stood over 395 feet high. Designed by the Greek architect Sostratos, it guided ships for about 1,500 years, and is considered to have been one of the Seven Wonders of the Ancient World.

Seeing within

Fiber optics have enabled advancements to take place in medicine, with a technique called "keyhole surgery." Endoscopy, which is the examination of the inside of the body by direct viewing, makes use of tubes with fiber-optic light sources and a lens at one end. Special tubes are used to view the blood vessels, lungs, and other hollow parts of the body. Minor surgery can also be done with these tubes, so that the patient does not have to be cut open. Forceps can be passed through an endoscope to obtain samples of tissue, and lasers can be inserted and used to destroy abnormal tissue.

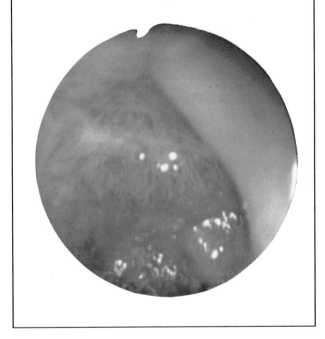

Long distance communication

Fiber-optic cables can carry sound and picture signals at high speed. During a telephone conversation, the light in the system flashes about 45 million times per second. Fiber-optics began carrying messages across the Atlantic in 1988, and across the Pacific Ocean in 1989.

The Anzcan cable links Sydney with Canada by way of Norfolk Island, Fiji, and Hawaii. It also has a spur to New Zealand. The Seacom cable links Cairns, Australia, with Hong Kong by way of Guam.

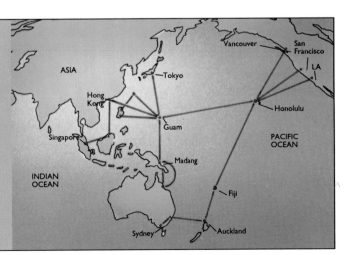

MILESTONES IN LIGHT

283-246 B.C.
During the reign of Ptolemy II in Egypt, the Greeks completed the Pharos of Alexandria – the tallest lighthouse ever built.

circa 10 B.C.
Candles have been used for over 2,000 years. They have been made from many substances, including beeswax and tallow.

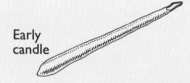

Early candle

A.D. 1590
A Dutch eyeglass maker, Zacharias Janssen, discovered the principle of the compound microscope.

1609
Galileo built his first telescope.

1665
Robert Hooke used his compound microscope to observe the structure of cork. He was the first to observe and name "little boxes," or cells.

1666
Sir Isaac Newton discovered that white light is made up of all colors.

1784
American scientist and statesman, Benjamin Franklin invented bifocals.

1826
French inventor Joseph Nicephore Niepce produced the world's first photograph using a camera obscura to give a permanent image.

1830s
French inventor, Louis Daguerre, produced the first sharp, detailed photographic image.

1852
Fluorescence was first explained by Sir George G. Stokes, a British physicist.

1879
Thomas A. Edison invented his incandescent lamp.

1888
George Eastman introduced the Kodak box camera.

1895
Wilhelm K. Roentgen, a German physicist, discovered x rays.

1896
American inventor, Thomas A. Edison improved the fluoroscope so it could be used to view x ray images.

1909
Solar power became a reality when William J. Bailey developed the first modern flat-plate collector in California.

1926
John Logie Baird demonstrated television, based on a mechanical method of scanning an image into lines of dots of light.

1960
The first laser was built by T. H. Maiman in the United States. It contained a specially made ruby rod.

1990
The Hubble Space Telescope was launched into orbit. Sensitive to both visible and ultraviolet light, flaws in the main mirror caused the telescope to produce slightly blurred images.

1992
The oldest light in the universe was discovered by the Cosmic Background Explorer satellite.

GLOSSARY

Concave Curving inward like a cave or the inside of a spoon.

Convex Curving outward like a ball.

Eclipse An eclipse occurs when one planet stops sunlight from reaching another.

Electromagnetic radiation Electric and magnetic forces which vibrate at right angles to each other and can travel through space. These include light, radio waves, and infrared and ultraviolet radiation.

Electromagnetic spectrum The complete range of known electromagnetic radiation, usually arranged in order of wavelength.

Fiber optics A way of sending light along very thin glass fibers.

Focus The point at which light rays come together to form a sharp, clear image.

Fluorescence A short-lived glow of light not caused by high temperature.

Hologram A ghostlike, three-dimensional picture normally produced by a laser.

Image The "picture" of an object produced by a mirror or a lens.

Laser A machine that can produce a narrow, powerful beam of light of one particular wavelength. The word "laser" stands for Light Amplification by Stimulated Emission of Radiation.

Lens A piece of transparent material with curved surfaces that bends or refracts light.

Optic nerve A long, stringlike structure that carries electrical messages from the back of the eye to the brain.

Photon The smallest particle of light energy.

Photosynthesis The process by which plants use the sun's energy to make their own food.

Pigment Any substance that gives color to plant or animal cells or can be ground up to a powder to color paints or dyes.

Prism A solid transparent shape usually made of glass, which can be used to separate the colors in visible light.

Reflection The bouncing back of light from a surface.

Refraction The bending of light when it passes from one transparent substance to another.

Retina The layer at the back of the eye that is sensitive to light. It contains rods and cones which are connected to the brain through the optic nerve.

Speed of light In air, light travels at 186,000 million miles per second, which is over 500,000 times faster than the Concorde. In solids or liquids, light travels more slowly.

Wavelength The length between identical points on two waves next to each other. Each type of electromagnetic radiation has a different wavelength.

INDEX

Photographic Credits:
All the pictures were taken by Roger Viltos apart from: front cover main picture: Dan Brooks; back cover bottom & pages 6 bottom, 16 middle & 23 bottom right: Bruce Coleman Ltd; 4 middle & bottom right: Hutchison Library; 4 bottom left, 26 bottom & 27 right: Frank Spooner Pictures; 7 top left: Paul Nightingale; 7 top right & bottom, 13 bottom, 18 bottom, 19 middle, 20 bottom right, 23 top & 29: Science Photo Library; 9 bottom, 13 top left & 23 bottom left: NHPA; 11 middle, 12 bottom left, 15 top right, 20 bottom left, 21 & 24-25 bottom: Mary Evans; 11 right: Hulton Picture Company; 12 bottom right, 13 middle & left & 28 right: Spectrum; 19 bottom: Science Museum, London; 22 top: Flick Killerby; 24-25 top: Archve Kunst; 26 top: McDonald Observatory, Texas.